POLAND

JEREMY NICHOLS AND
EMILIA TREMBICKA-NICHOLS

Facts On File, Inc.

TITLES IN THE COUNTRIES OF THE WORLD SERIES:

ARGENTINA • AUSTRALIA • BRAZIL • CANADA • CHINA
EGYPT • FRANCE • GERMANY • INDIA • ITALY • JAPAN
KENYA • MEXICO • NIGERIA • POLAND • UNITED KINGDOM
UNITED STATES • VIETNAM

Poland

Facts On File, Inc.
132 West 31st Street
New York NY 10001

Library of Congress Cataloging-in-Publication Data

Nichols, Jeremy, 1966–
    Poland / Jeremy Nichols and Emilia Trembicka-Nichols.
       p. cm. — (Countries of the world)
    Includes bibliographical references and index.
    ISBN 0-8160-6005-3
    1. Poland—Juvenile literature. I. Trembicka-Nichols,
Emilia, 1969– II. Title. III. Countries of the world (Facts
On File, Inc.)
    DK4147.N53 2005
    943.8—dc22
                    2005040680

Facts On File books are available at special discounts when purchased in bulk quantities for businesses, associations, institutions, or sales promotions. Please call our Special Sales Department in New York at (212) 967-8800 or (800) 322-8755.

You can find Facts On File on the World Wide Web at http://www.factsonfile.com.

Printed in China by Leo Paper Products Ltd.

10 9 8 7 6 5 4 3 2 1

Editor: Daniel Rogers
Designer: Mayer Media, Ltd.
Picture researchers: Lynda Lines and Frances Bailey
Map artwork: Peter Bull
Charts and graphs: Encompass Graphics, Ltd.

Photograph acknowledgments
All by Richard Laing except: 14 bottom (Forum/Andrzej Sidor, Reuters); 15, 22 top, 34, 41 top, 50 (Piotr Malecki, Rainbow); 16 top (Jerry Bergman, Rex Features); 17, 18, 47 top (Pawel Kopczynski, Reuters); 27 bottom (Avikainen, Rex Features); 31, 36 bottom (Imagia, Link Picture Agency); 33, 37, 38 bottom (Transit Archiv/Peter Hirth, Still Pictures); 52 (Peter Jordan, Network Photographers); 53 top (Piotr Gesicki, Rainbow); 57 top (Nikola Solic, Reuters).

First published by Evans Brothers Limited,
2A Portman Mansions, Chiltern Street,
London W1U 6NR, United Kingdom.

This edition published under license from Evans Brothers Limited. All rights reserved.

Endpapers (front): The docks at the shipyard in Gdansk, with work in progress.
Title page: A street scene in Zakopane, a popular mountain resort.
Imprint and Contents pages: Farmland and open countryside around the town of Swiecko in southwest Poland.
Endpapers (back): Rybi Potok, a mountain stream in the Tatras.

CONTENTS

The Polish flag consists of two horizontal bands in the state colors, white and red.

The fourteenth-century Cloth Hall in Cracow's main square.

Poland is a large and varied country, with a long and eventful history, rich in natural and created treasures. It has undergone rapid change since the late 1980s. The results of these changes are plainly visible today, particularly in the cities. However, there are also many aspects of Poland and Polish life that have remained unchanged for centuries.

PROVINCES OF POLAND

In Poland you can find busy cities, ancient castles, modern hotels, efficient railways, and international airports, as well as bison, wolves, farmers using horse-drawn plows, ornate cathedrals, Internet cafés, chic art galleries, bustling street markets and storks nesting on chimney tops.

The country has areas of great natural beauty, including high mountain ranges, large forests and a long, sandy coastline. Nearly a third of the country is covered by forest. It has a huge area of farmland, which makes up more than half of Poland's total landmass.

Poland also has a vibrant cultural and artistic life, and above all it has warm, friendly and hospitable people.

Poland joined the European Union in 2004, but in reality it has always been a key European country. In the twentieth century, Poland was the flash point for World War II, and also the place where a political and social movement started the downfall of Communism in Poland and then in neighboring countries. Since this sudden change in 1989, Poland's economy has developed rapidly. This has brought a new dynamism and energy to the country and has also made some social contrasts more marked than before.

The Poles themselves are a religious people, and more than 90 percent of the population are Roman Catholic. While the church is gradually becoming less important to younger people, it has been a powerful force in Polish life for a very long time. Before 1989, the Catholic Church, with its charismatic Polish Pope, John Paul II, played a vital role in the social and political movements that eventually brought an end to the Communist regime. There are countless churches, cathedrals and examples of religious art in Poland.

In the worlds of business, industry and commerce, Poland is moving away from its heavily industrialized past and is modernizing many areas of its economy. It is also making great strides in the fields of environmental protection and conservation.

KEY DATA

Official Name:	Republic of Poland
Area:	312,685km^2
Population:	38,626,349 (2004 est.)
Official Language:	Polish
Main Cities:	Warsaw (capital), Cracow, Gdansk, Lodz, Poznan, Wroclaw
GDP Per Capita:	US$11,100*
Currency:	zloty (PLN)
Exchange Rate:	US$1 = 3.16 PLN €1 = 4.10 PLN

*(2004) Calculated on Purchasing Power Parity basis.
Sources: *CIA World Factbook, 2004*; World Bank; UN Human Development Report, 2003

A typical view of farmland in Kujawsko-Pomorskie, one of the main cereal-growing regions.

The Polish gun emplacement at Westerplatte, starting point of the 1939 Nazi invasion, which still bears the marks of the attack.

EARLY HISTORY

There is evidence of human settlement in what is now Poland dating back 30,000 years, but it was in A.D. 966 that the country's first recorded ruler, Duke Mieszko I, converted to Christianity. This marked the beginning of the Piast dynasty, which ruled until 1370.

In general terms, Poland has Eastern European (Slavonic) roots and has absorbed Western European (particularly Roman Catholic) influences through the centuries.

The seventeenth and eighteenth centuries saw many wars and a Swedish invasion known in Polish as *Potop* ("the Deluge"). By 1795 Poland had been partitioned (divided up) among Russia, Prussia (Germany) and Austria. Afterward Poland disappeared from the map for more than 120 years.

1918–1945

Poland regained its independence at the end of World War I in 1918, under Marshal Jozef Pilsudski. This lasted until Germany invaded Poland on 1 September 1939, sparking World War II. The Soviet Union then invaded eastern Poland on 17 September 1939, following the terms of an agreement with Nazi Germany to divide Poland between them.

Poland suffered some of the worst atrocities of the war. Many Poles were executed; the Nazi leader Adolf Hitler ordered the total destruction of Warsaw and its Jewish population; and Nazi death camps were built on Polish soil. Between 1 million and 2 million Poles were exiled by Soviet forces between 1939 and 1941.

SOVIET COMMUNISM

At the end of World War II in 1945, Poland came under the rule of the communist Soviet Union. Poland was forced to give up a large amount (180,000km^2) of its eastern territory to Russia, but it also regained territory (100,000km^2) from Germany in the west. In 1948 the communist Polish United Workers' Party (PZPR) was formed, and a Soviet-style constitution was introduced in 1952. There were strikes in 1956 and 1970 in protest against economic conditions, but these were put down by force.

In 1980 strikes organized by the Solidarity labor union spread across the country, and on 13 December 1981 General Wojciech Jaruzelski imposed martial law. Travel was restricted and many political activists were jailed.

THE NEW ORDER

In 1989 the political struggle led to roundtable discussions, starting in February and ending in agreements signed on 5 April. Free elections followed in 1990, and Solidarity became the new government of a democratic and independent Poland.

After 1989 the pace of development was very swift, as Poland began the change to a free-market economy. With the imposition of tight economic controls, the economy thrived.

Since 1989 Poland has been a democracy, with an elected 460-seat *Sejm* (Parliament), a 100-seat *Senat* (Senate) and an elected president. Lech Walesa, the leader of Solidarity, was president from 1991 to 1995, followed by Aleksander Kwasniewski of the SLD Party.

In 1999 Poland took a significant step toward a new role in world affairs when it became a member of NATO. More recently, in May 2004, Poland was one of 10 countries to join the European Union (EU), bringing the benefits of membership and trade, travel and work opportunities to Poles throughout Europe.

Poland is divided into 16 regions called *wojewodztwa* (singular *wojewodztwo*). Each is divided into districts called *powiaty*, and these are divided into parishes or municipalities called *gminy*. Local governors and assemblies run the local districts.

The Palac Kultury, once a symbol of Soviet domination, still shapes Warsaw's skyline.

CASE STUDY
SOLIDARITY

Following widespread strikes in August 1980, Polish workers won the right to have an independent labor union. Solidarity, the first such union in a Soviet-bloc country, was formed on 22 September 1980 in Gdansk. When General Jaruzelski's government tried to crush Solidarity by declaring martial law in December 1981, the union continued to work as an underground organization until its legalization again in 1989 and historic election victory in 1990. Solidarity still continues today, but its political influence is far less than it was in the 1980s.

The Solidarity Memorial in Gdansk stands outside the old shipyard gates.

The High Tatras, seen beyond some examples of the local architectural style.

Poland is located in the heart of Europe, on the North European Plain. It is bordered by the Baltic Sea to the north and northwest; by Germany to the west; by Ukraine, Belarus, Russia and Lithuania to the east and northeast; and by Slovakia and the Czech Republic to the south. In general, Poland is mountainous in the south, with the terrain becoming increasingly flatter toward the north.

LANDSCAPE FEATURES

MOUNTAINS

The mountains in the south form several ranges. The Carpathian Mountains, to the east, include the highest range of all, the Tatras. The tallest peak in the Tatras is Mt Rysy, at 2,499m. The Tatras are the most scenic mountains in Poland. Rocky and snow-capped, they are visually stunning and attract many walkers, climbers and tourists. The Carpathian range also includes the Bieszczady Mountains to the southeast. The highest point here is Mt Tarnica, at 1,343m.

West of the Carpathians are the lower Sudeten Mountains, which are some of the oldest mountains in Europe. They lie along the border with the Czech Republic, and their highest peak is Mt Sniezka, at 1,602m. These mountains are made of sandstone of varying density and hardness lying in horizontal layers. They have been formed into a plateau structure by millions of years of weathering, which has also created unusual rock formations including natural labyrinths (mazes). The slopes of the Stolowe Mountains, in the middle range of the Sudeten Mountains, are covered with forests and meadows.

This area has a very specific and quite harsh climate, with a short summer and a winter with very heavy snowfalls.

North of the Tatra range is the lower but much larger Beskid range, with its highest peak, Mt Babia Gora, at 1,725m. This range is heavily forested.

The gently sloping Stolowe Mountains, in the Sudeten range.

This farmer is planting potatoes near Legnica in Silesia.

UPLANDS AND PLAIN

Farther north, the terrain drops to form the uplands of Malopolska (Little Poland) and Upper Silesia. This is a region of rolling hills and valleys. The coal-rich, heavily populated and industrialized region of Upper Silesia is centered on the city of Katowice. In Malopolska, the Cracow-Czestochowa Upland was formed from limestone around 150 million years ago, and erosion has left behind unusual rock formations and hundreds of caves.

Still farther north, the uplands give way to the large, low-lying central plain that stretches in a wide east-to-west band across the country. This belt is the agricultural heartland of Poland and comprises the regions of Wielkopolskie, Dolnoslaskie, Kujawsko-Pomorskie, Mazowieckie and Podlaskie. Much of the land here is farmland, and these regions produce most of Poland's cereal crops.

In the northern part of the country, the central plain rises to become more undulating terrain, interspersed with lakes. This part of Poland is often called the Baltic Heights.

The tranquil lakes of Mazuria are ideal for boaters of all kinds.

THE LAKE DISTRICT

The region of Mazuria (or Mazurskie) in northeast Poland is often called Poland's Lake District. Poland has more than 9,000 lakes in all, and roughly 3,000 of them are in Mazuria. In the central part more than 15 percent of the total area is water. Poland's two largest lakes are to be found here – Sniardwy (114km^2), and the Mamry (104km^2), which is in fact several lakes joined together including Lake Mamry itself. All the larger lakes are linked by rivers or canals to make a continuous network. This forested, sparsely populated area extends right up to the border with Lithuania. The region of Warmia, stretching from the north of Mazuria to Russia, is geographically very similar to Mazuria.

NATIONAL PARKS

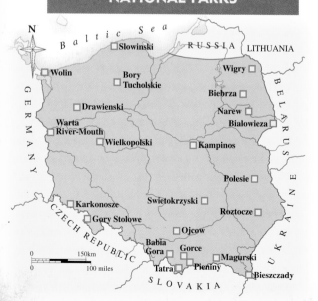

One of the best known of Poland's 23 National Parks is Bialowieza National Park, on the eastern border with Belarus. The total area of the park is more than 10,000 hectares, and more than 90 percent of this is covered by forest. Bialowieza started as a *rezerwat* (reserve) in 1921, and is one of the oldest national parks in Europe. It is home to about 12,000 species of animals, birds and insects, including a herd of more than 250 wild European bison – the only ones on the continent. Other animals to be found here include the lynx, wolf and beaver. There is a strict preservation order in one area of the park, where some of the oak trees are more than 400 years old. Bialowieza National Park was designated a UNESCO World Heritage Site in 1979.

Bison in the Bialowieza National Park can be seen in their natural habitat.

POMERANIA

In northwestern Poland, directly west of Mazuria, lies Pomerania. More varied than Mazuria, this region includes a long stretch of coastline, part of the lower Vistula River valley, and lakeland between the Vistula valley and the German border. The Vistula valley area is mostly agricultural and fairly level. In the west, around 50km from the Oder River, which marks the border with Germany, the lakes and forests dwindle and the land level drops. This area is known as the Szczecin Lowland.

THE COAST

Poland's coastline, along the Baltic Sea, is 524km long. The coast is mostly straight and flat, but there are also gently hilly and wooded parts. There are many long beaches between Gdansk and Germany. Near Leba, in the Slowinski National Park, is a mass of shifting sand dunes. The dunes consist of pale sand thrown up by the sea, which is dried by the wind and then blown inland, forming a ridge more than 30m high. The dunes are moving inland at a speed of around 10m per year, killing all vegetation in their path. Along this part of the coast are many lakes, separated from the sea by spits of sand. These lakes were originally sea bays, and are very shallow.

THE BALTIC

The Baltic Sea itself is calm, quite shallow and practically tideless. The countries that border the Baltic are Poland, Russia, Estonia, Lithuania, Latvia, Finland, Sweden, Denmark and Germany. Because the tides are weak, industrial pollution released in varying amounts from these countries has built up in the Baltic over the years. This situation is improving, however, as countries are addressing the problem.

In summer, favorite Baltic beaches can get crowded, like this one at Leba.

RIVERS

There are two major rivers in Poland, the Vistula and the Oder. Nearly all of Poland is drained northward into the Baltic by these two rivers and their tributaries.

THE VISTULA

The Vistula begins in the Beskid Mountains and ends in a delta at the Baltic coast, in the Gulf of Gdansk. It flows for 1,069km in a long S-shape, passing through two of Poland's major cities – Cracow (or Krakow) and Warsaw – before emerging close to Gdansk.

The Vistula Basin – the area of land that is drained by the river and its tributaries – covers most of eastern Poland. Rivers that join the Vistula in this basin include the Dunajec, a mountain river in the Tatras, and the Bug. For 280km of its length, the Bug forms Poland's border with Ukraine and Belarus before joining the Vistula north of Warsaw.

Because it flows the whole length of Poland and ends in a small sea surrounded by several other countries, the Vistula was for centuries a vital trade route for the Poles. In fact, in the sixteenth century, the grain trade in Poland was known as the Vistula Trade. The river was used extensively for transport until recent times.

The Oder River near Szczecin, one of Poland's main ports.

THE ODER

The Oder River rises in the Czech Republic and crosses into Polish territory near Raciborz in the south of Poland. It then flows northward for 742km, reaching the Baltic Sea at the port of Szczecin. For part of its length it forms Poland's border with Germany. The Oder's main tributaries are the Warta and Notec Rivers. The Warta begins in Upper Silesia, and the basin formed by the Oder and Warta together drains the western part of Poland.

Apart from Szczecin, the other important city on the banks of the Oder is Wroclaw, the fourth-largest city in Poland.

The Vistula River flows through Warsaw, with the center of the city on its western side.

RIVER DRAINAGE

Despite these major rivers and their tributaries, the drainage of much of Poland is poor. This is because a lot of the terrain is level, and extensive marshlands and, particularly in the north, small lakes have formed.

The rivers have two annual high-water periods. The first is caused by snow and ice melting in spring, and the second by heavy rainfall, usually in July. Occasionally, this second period can bring severe flooding.

CASE STUDY
FLOODS

In July 1997, following extensive heavy rain, southwest Poland experienced one of the worst floods in its history. Water covered 10 percent of the whole country. More than 50 people were killed, many more were injured and around 3 million were badly affected. More than 200 bridges were washed away, and roads, buildings (including hospitals), industries and sewage systems were severely damaged. Water works were flooded and electricity supplies were interrupted. Worst hit was Wroclaw, on the banks of the Oder River. It was more than a month before the city had its normal water supply back.

A man wades across a flooded street in the center of Wroclaw, July 1997.

All flooded crops were declared unfit for consumption because of raw sewage in the floodwater, and many cattle and other animals died. Operations by the military and rescue services involved 35,000 men, 76 helicopters and 387 boats, and many volunteers also helped. After the floods, Poland started a flood-management project with assistance from Denmark and the World Bank. This project included setting up systems for more accurate flood forecasting as well as structural protection measures.

CLIMATE

Poland has a cool temperate climate with a combination of maritime and continental climatic patterns. Because these two patterns meet over Poland, there are as many as six different seasons, with wide regional variations in the weather.

Humid air from the Atlantic moves across Poland from the west and dry air from Eurasia moves in from the east. As a result, western Poland tends to be wetter and milder than eastern Poland.

SEASONS

This combination of weather systems also means that the seasons reach Poland from different directions. Spring weather comes mainly from the west, autumn and winter from the east, and summer from the south.

As well as the usual four seasons, Poland has two distinct extra ones – an "early spring" and an "early winter." During these periods of change before and after winter, average temperatures stay between 0°C and 5°C.

Spring in Poland usually lasts around 60 days, with average temperatures between 5°C and 15°C. Summer starts in May and lasts until September. Then there is often an "Indian summer," a warm and sunny period of autumn before early winter starts. After a few weeks of early winter, true winter begins in November and lasts through to March.

The seasons have different lengths in different parts of the country. For example, in Silesia in the southwest, winters are quite mild, lasting 70 to 80 days on average, and summers are long and warm, while in northeastern Poland summer is often warm too, but winter can be more than four months long and bitterly cold.

TEMPERATURES

In the upland areas of Pomerania and Mazuria the average annual temperature is 5°C to 7°C. Farther south, in Silesia and Wielkopolskie, this rises to 8°C to 10°C. In the High Tatras,

Heavy snow in southern Poland makes a horse-drawn sleigh a useful means of travel.

Baltic sailors take advantage of the coastal breezes.

however, the average drops to around 0°C. The hottest month is July, with an average of 16°C to 19°C, and the temperature can climb higher than 25°C. It is cooler in the mountains and nearer the sea. The coldest month is January, with temperatures decreasing across the country from west to east. The average number of days below freezing ranges from 90 per year by the sea to more than 200 per year in the mountains.

The highest recorded temperature in Poland was 40.2°C in Pruszkow in 1921, and the lowest was –41°C in Siedlce in 1940.

CLOUDS, RAIN AND SNOW

During the year, 60 to 70 percent of the days are cloudy, though the clouds do not always bring rain or snow. The most overcast month is November, and the least cloudy months are August and September.

Annual rainfall is between 400 and 750mm in the lowlands and uplands, and 800 to 1,400mm in the mountains. The heaviest rainfall occurs in summer – June is the wettest month – and, except in the mountains, it is least likely to rain in February. Summer rainfall is around two to three times higher than in winter.

It snows on average for 30 to 40 days a year in western and central Poland, for more than 50 days in the northeast, and 145 days in the Tatras.

WINDS

Winds in Poland are generally weak or moderate, with speeds of between 7 and 36 km/h, though there can be stronger winds at the coast and in the mountains.

There are regional variations too, such as the Baltic Sea breezes and the *halny* wind in the mountains. The *halny* is strong and gusty, bringing higher temperatures and lower humidity. It can be strong enough to knock down trees.

TEMPERATURE AND RAINFALL

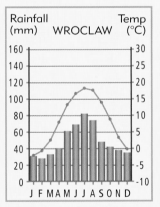

Rainfall (mm)   WROCLAW   Temp (°C)

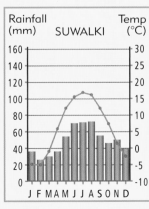

Rainfall (mm)   SUWALKI   Temp (°C)

KEY:

Temperature   Rainfall

Residential buildings in Przymorze, Gdansk – the longest such complex in Europe.

Poland's population has grown considerably since 1945, but it is now very stable and is even showing signs of starting to fall slightly. The population is mostly native Polish, with a few significant ethnic minority groups (see pages 22–23).

POPULATION GROWTH

Poland currently has a population of around 38.6 million people.

In the years following World War II, the population rose sharply, from nearly 25 million in 1950 to more than 32 million in 1970. In the mid-1950s, the annual growth rate peaked at 2 percent. Between 1965 and 1984, the growth rate was slower and quite steady, at an average of 0.9 percent per year.

Since the mid-1980s, however, the rate has dropped year by year until, in the years from 1998 to 2001, the population remained practically constant.

The census of 2002 actually shows a drop in the population of 0.1 percent compared with the previous year, and this trend is predicted to continue in the coming decades. One reason for this is the relatively large proportion of the population that is over 60 years of age.

POPULATION STRUCTURE

The ratio of males to females in the population varies depending on the age group, but overall the balance is 48.5 percent males to 51.5 percent females. In the younger age groups (up to 15 years) the ratio is roughly 51:49, and between 15 and 64

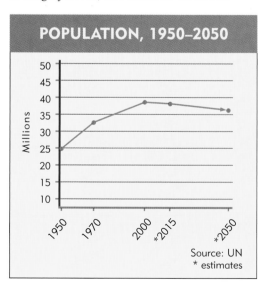

POPULATION, 1950–2050

Millions

Source: UN
* estimates

years it is almost exactly 50:50, but at age 65 and above it swings to 38:62, because women tend to live longer than men. The average life expectancy is 74 years in Poland – 70 for men and 78 for women.

Grouped by age, 17.5 percent of the Polish population are 14 years old or younger, 69.8 percent are between 15 and 64, and 12.7 percent are 65 and over.

POPULATION DISTRIBUTION AND DENSITY

One of the most significant changes in the distribution of Poland's population took place in the first two decades of Soviet rule, between 1945 and 1965, when there was a period of intensive urbanization. The centralized economic planning of Communism played a part in this, and there was a large movement of people away from rural areas and into the towns.

Although the flow of people to the cities had slowed by the late 1970s, today 62 percent of Poles live in urban areas. This figure is predicted to increase to 64 percent by 2015.

The average population density in Poland is 124 people per square kilometer, but it varies from place to place. The most densely populated areas are Warsaw and the city of Katowice in the southwest, including the extended urban region surrounding it. Warsaw has a population of around 1.7 million, but including the surrounding urban area raises this to nearly 2.5 million. Katowice itself has a population of 329,000, but with the surrounding urban districts this climbs to almost 3 million.

The northern areas of the country, and particularly the northeastern territories around the city of Suwalki, are much less densely populated.

Poland has more than 20 cities with populations of at least 150,000 people. The top five in order of size, and not counting the area around Katowice, are Warsaw, Lodz, Cracow, Wroclaw and Poznan.

POPULATION STRUCTURE, 2004

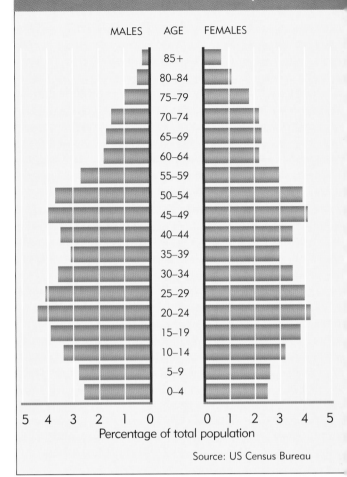

Source: US Census Bureau

POPULATION DENSITY

Population per km²
- 400 and over
- 101–399
- 61–100
- 0–60

POPULATION AND NATIONALITY

The population of Poland today is mostly made up of native Poles. In the national census that was conducted in 2002, 96.7 percent of the people stated that they consider themselves to be Polish. Of the rest, 1.23 percent (471,500 people) declared another nationality, and 2.03 percent (774,900 people) did not declare any nationality.

The Poles are part of an ethnic group called the West Slavs, which also includes Czech and Slovakian peoples. The East Slavs include Russians, Belarusians and Ukrainians, while the South Slav peoples inhabit Bulgaria, Slovenia, Macedonia and the Balkan countries. The same broad division can be applied to the languages of these groups. Polish itself is a Slavonic language written, like Western European languages, using the Roman alphabet.

A member of Warsaw's Jewish community in front of a synagogue.

A Vietnamese restaurateur proudly shows the interior of his Cracow restaurant.

OTHER ETHNICITY

There are several other ethnic groups living in Poland. Although they are native to Poland, many Silesians and Kashubians do not regard themselves as Polish. The Kashubians – who live in an area southwest of Gdansk – speak a different language and have their own traditions and culture.

The largest foreign minority in Poland are Germans, mostly living in Silesia, Pomerania and Warmia. The number of Poles claiming German descent rose sharply after the political changes of the early 1990s, when it became easier for people living in former German regions to be more open about their origins.

Before World War II, there were 3.3 million Jews in Poland – the largest Jewish community in the world. In the 2002 census, only 1,100 people stated that they were Jewish, though the true figure is thought to be higher than this, at between 5,000 and 10,000 people. Many Polish Jews live in Warsaw and Wroclaw.

Another significant minority are the Vietnamese. Links between Poland and Vietnam developed partly from student exchange programs during the Communist era, which allowed Vietnamese students to study in Poland. Economic conditions at the beginning of the 1990s encouraged such students and former students to stay and start small businesses in Poland. Their friends and families often followed. The Polish government claims there are now up to 50,000 Vietnamese immigrants in Poland, though Vietnamese community leaders claim the true figure is about half that size. Most live in Warsaw, where there are 300 to 400 Vietnamese fast-food restaurants and 30 or so large restaurants.

EMIGRATION

It is estimated that up to 20 million Poles live outside Poland – more than half the population of Poland itself. Of these, roughly 10 million live in the United States. Poles often say that Chicago is the second-largest Polish city in the world, since it has the highest Polish population after Warsaw. It is possible to live and work in Chicago's Polish district and speak nothing but Polish.

Germany is home to around 1.6 million Poles, and there are another million in both Brazil and France. Poles live in more than 90 countries of the world. There have been three significant waves of emigration in the last hundred years: at the beginning of the twentieth century, during and after World War II, and following the imposition of martial law in 1981–84 (when Poles traveling abroad could not return to Poland because the government prohibited it). The net emigration rate was between 10,000 and 20,000 people per year from 1990 to 2002.

Recent high unemployment in Poland has prompted a larger number of graduates and professionals to look for opportunities outside the country.

Heading west – a checkpoint on the Polish-German border.

RELIGION

More than 90 percent of Poles have a religious faith, and over 50 percent practice their faith regularly by attending services. The Roman Catholic Church has the largest number of members – more than 25 million – and it has been a fundamental part of Polish life since the beginnings of the Polish state. There are three other types of Catholicism in Poland – Byzantine-Ukrainian, Neo-Uniate, and Armenian.

The Catholic Church played an important role in the social and political movements that led to the end of Communism. The Church's influence was strengthened by the appointment in 1978 of a Polish Pope, John Paul II (born Karol Wojtyla).

The second-largest religious group in Poland is the Polish Orthodox Church, with around half a million members. Most are found in the Belarusian communities of eastern Poland.

There are also several branches of Protestantism in the country. The largest, the Augsburg Evangelical Church, has more than 85,000 members.

A street procession during the Corpus Christi festival in Rumia, near Gdynia.

Many other religious groups can be found in Poland, including the Union of Jewish Religious Communities (Judaism) and the Muslim Religious Union (Islam). In all, there are 138 registered churches and religious groups in Poland.

There are many great examples of cathedrals, churches and religious art in Poland, and many Christian religious holidays and festivals take place during the year. Corpus Christi in June is a particularly important Christian festival, celebrated with colorful street processions.

EDUCATION

Since 1999 the Polish education system has undergone extensive reforms. Education is now compulsory up to the age of 18 and all state education is free.

Preprimary school, for children ages three to six, is optional, though most six-year-olds complete a year of preparation before going to primary school.

Primary school lasts for six years, from ages seven to 13. In the first three years, all subjects are taught by one class teacher. During the next three years, specialist teachers teach different subjects.

At the age of 13, students attend a three-year lower secondary school, which leads to examinations at age 16.

The minaret of a mosque reaches skyward in Przymorze, Gdansk.

Students enjoying the sunshine at the Jagiellonian University in Cracow.

CASE STUDY
LODZ FILM SCHOOL

The National Film, Television and Theater School was set up in Lodz in 1948. Lodz was the nearest large city to Warsaw (which had been largely destroyed during World War II), so many artists went there to work.

From the beginning there have been two main departments in the school – film directing and cinematography. Other departments include film editing, screenwriting and sound technology. The theater school joined the film school in 1958, and the acting department works closely with the filmmakers. The combined school has trained several famous directors, including Roman Polanski, Andrzej Wajda and Krzysztof Kieslowski.

Students then either go to a general upper secondary school for three years, a technical school for four years, or a vocational school for two to three years. Upper secondary and technical school studies end with the *matura*, an exit exam. In 2005, the *matura* became the standard qualification needed to enter universities and colleges. At this higher level, students study for a licentiate (usually involving three years' study) or a master's degree, which takes five to six years.

The number of students in higher education in Poland has been growing in recent years, mainly because the number of places available has increased. In 2001 there were 1,584,800 students in full-time study – nearly four times as many as 10 years earlier.

HEALTH

The Polish health care system has also undergone reforms since the 1980s. The system is now paid for by personal health insurance instead of taxes. Life expectancy in Poland is increasing, but the birth rate has decreased. Although the death rate from heart disease has fallen since the 1980s, the rate from lung cancer is still quite high, mainly because many older Poles are smokers.

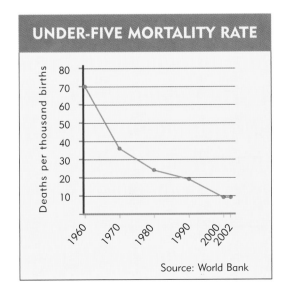

UNDER-FIVE MORTALITY RATE

Source: World Bank

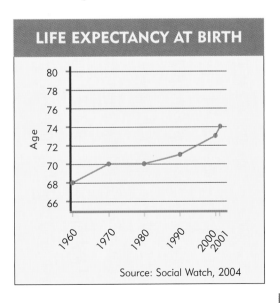

LIFE EXPECTANCY AT BIRTH

Source: Social Watch, 2004

A farmer using a horse-drawn plow – a common sight in rural Poland.

Nearly two thirds of Poland's total area is farmland, and more than 20 percent of the working population is employed in agriculture. While not all of them work in farming full-time, around 2 million Polish people currently earn their main living on farms.

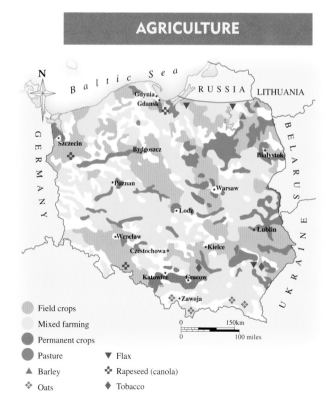

AGRICULTURE

- Field crops
- Mixed farming
- Permanent crops
- Pasture
- ▲ Barley
- ❖ Oats
- ▼ Flax
- ❖ Rapeseed (canola)
- ◆ Tobacco

0   150km
0   100 miles

FARM SIZE

Agriculture was one of the few areas of the economy to remain largely unaffected by the Soviet system. Most farms stayed in private hands during the Communist era, instead of being collectivized into larger state-owned farms. Collectivization was attempted after the war, but farmers strongly resisted it. Production suffered badly, and when the moderate Communist Party leader Wladyslaw Gomulka came to power in 1956 he reversed the policy. As a result, there are now more than 2 million individual farms in Poland. The farms that did become state-owned, called PGRs, all went bankrupt in the 1990s.

Privately owned farms in Poland are typically not very large. In 2002, 32 percent of all farms were 1 hectare (about the size of a football field) or less, and another 38 percent were between 1 and

5 hectares. Less than 5 percent were larger than 30 hectares.

Many small farms are inefficient by modern standards, but they are environmentally friendly. Often a farmer will keep a couple of cows, a pig, possibly a horse, and some ducks and chickens as well as cultivating a small area. Pesticides and fertilizers are not used much on such farms.

Large-scale farming operations are still not common in Poland, but the larger, more technologically advanced farms are found mostly in the west of the country.

LABOR FORCE

Around 90 percent of people employed in agriculture work on their own farms. Men make up 55 percent of the workforce and women 45 percent. Many farmers continue working after the official retirement age, which is 65 for men and 60 for women. More than 12 percent of the agricultural workforce is past retirement age; in other industries the figure is less than 2 percent.

CROPS AND LIVESTOCK

The main crops grown in Poland are cereals (including wheat, oats, corn and rye), potatoes, sugar beet, rapeseed (canola), turnips, fruit and many types of vegetables. Cereals account for 75 percent of the sown area of Polish farmland, and potatoes another 7 percent. Strawberry and black currant plantations are also common.

Farmworkers making hay in summer, near Pisz in Mazuria.

Pigs are the most numerous livestock animals in Poland, at more than 18.5 million animals. Cattle make up the next largest number – 5.5 million – followed by much smaller numbers of sheep, goats and horses.

There are also around 200 million poultry birds in Poland and some 500,000 beehives producing honey. Forest products, such as wild mushrooms and berries, are important additional crops.

Finally, there is a strong tradition of horse breeding in Poland, and the country is particularly famous for producing world-class Arabian thoroughbreds.

Pig farming is one of the mainstays of Polish agriculture. More intensive methods are now being introduced.

MODERNIZATION AND RESTRUCTURING

The agricultural and food production sector in Poland currently employs nearly 30 percent of the workforce but contributes only 4 percent to the country's gross domestic product (GDP).

This low productivity is mainly because of the way farmland is owned and managed. About 2 million farms are in private hands and 70 percent are 5 hectares or smaller. This means that much produce is grown for the owners' own use and never reaches the market. These small farms account for around 90 percent of Poland's total food production,

This modern greenhouse in Mazuria houses a thriving tomato crop.

but it is estimated that only 47 percent of them produce food for sale.

This pattern has been common in rural Poland for centuries, and most farmers have no desire to change. However, many also earn income through other work, and if there were a more diverse rural economy, more farmers might be willing to change careers. Unemployment in rural regions is high, making up 44 percent of Poland's total figure.

CHANGES IN LAND USE (HECTARES), 1996–2002

	1996	2002	% CHANGE
Area of agricultural holdings	20.8 million ha	19.3 million ha	−6.9%
Sown area	12.3 million ha	10.8 million ha	−12.5%
Orchards	249.3 thousand ha	271 thousand ha	+8.7%
Nonagricultural land	11.35 million ha	11.9 million ha	+4.6%

Source: Polish Agricultural Census, 2002

In addition to these issues, Poland has been working to meet the requirements of European Union (EU) membership relating to productivity, efficiency, and health and safety in farming and food production.

Recent government policy has had three main aims: making agriculture more profitable and competitive; developing economic activities in rural area; and bringing the sector into line with EU laws and institutions.

CONSOLIDATION OF LAND USE

In some places, smaller farms are being merged to make them larger and more efficient, but there is not enough land available for sale to make this possible across the country.

This is because small farmers are reluctant to move away from rural areas or to change their employment, partly because of the costs involved. For such a farmer, the process of selling the farm, moving to a city and taking a manufacturing job, for example, would be simply too expensive because of the higher cost of housing in the cities.

The large state farms of the Communist period, which went bankrupt in the 1990s, are now mostly leased to tenant farmers. The tenants have been unable to purchase them because they lack access to credit.

A fully mechanized farming operation – imported Danish combine harvesters on a large farm near Poznan.

FOREIGN INVESTMENT

In the last 15 years foreign investment in Poland's agricultural and food-processing sector has been substantial – about US$20 billion in total. Large-scale meat producers, such as the US company Smithfield, and supermarket chains, such as the French company Auchan, have set up major operations in Poland and intend to expand them. Companies such as Smithfield are introducing more intensive farming methods.

ORGANIC FARMING

Polish farmers have traditionally used very few pesticides and chemical fertilizers, so one obvious way for Polish agriculture to develop is into organic food production. Organic farming offers a good opportunity for small farmers to increase their revenues, because organic products sell at a higher prices and demand for them is increasing across Europe. Many small farms are already moving in this direction. However, in order to be able to sell their produce as organic in the European Union, farms need to have been certified for two to three years. Polish farmers were reluctant to apply for certification before Poland was an EU member, and farmers who applied recently have to wait before they can export their produce as organic.

This Auchan hypermarket is one example of foreign investment in the food sector.

These foods processed in Poland are bound for the United Kingdom, another EU member.

MARKETS AND EXPORTS

In 2003 more than 50 percent of Polish food exports went to EU countries (including the nine other countries that joined the European Union in the following year, at the same time as Poland). Total food exports are worth more than US$30 billion per year. Germany takes the largest share, at around 30 percent of the total, with Italy, France, the United Kingdom and the Czech Republic taking 4 to 6 percent each. Russia, the United States and Canada are also significant export partners. Poland's main exports are rapeseed (canola), candies, meat, fruit and vegetables.

Freight containers being loaded onto a ship at night, from the container terminal at Gdynia docks.

EU MEMBERSHIP

In the period leading up to EU membership in 2004, Poland received assistance from the European Union and the World Bank to help bring its agriculture into line with European standards, and to develop its rural infrastructure. EU agricultural planning focuses on productivity and efficiency, and Poland has to make great changes to its farming system to meet EU goals. However, Poland's farmers, who have worked the same land for many generations, oppose large-scale farming. In response to the idea of merging small family farms into larger units, Polish farmers will often refer to their resistance to the Communist attempt at collectivization in the 1940s and 1950s. While some farms will expand in future, many others will probably remain small but will diversify into such areas as agrotourism and organic farming.

EU rules on food production and processing are strict, and many food-processing operations have had to modernize and change. There have been marked improvements in these areas. For example, before 1990 only 6 percent of milk produced in Poland was acceptable for export to EU countries.

A modern Polish food-processing factory. Businesses that process meat products must meet high standards.

By 2004 the figure was 65 percent. A similar pattern can be seen in pork manufacturing.

The European Commission has given many producers until 2006 to meet EU norms, and these companies will not be able to export within the European Union until then. It is likely that many food production companies will be forced to close, however, which will mean heavy job losses.

The European Union funds some farms through its Common Agricultural Policy (CAP). There has been much debate about how much financial subsidy Polish farmers should get. Because so many Polish farms are small and unprofitable, some other EU members have argued that they should not get the same amount of funding as larger, more efficient farms in other member states. CAP funding will be reviewed in 2006.

POLISH LEGISLATION

In some areas of agricultural production, existing Polish regulations are stricter than the new EU ones. For example, Polish law permits fewer preservatives to be used in food, and the use of hormonal growth stimulants for animals is prohibited.

ENERGY CROPS

A new area of agriculture in Poland is that of growing crops for producing energy. Rapeseed is the plant most commonly used for this purpose, as rapeseed oil can be converted into biogas as an energy source. Poland is already a major producer of this crop, and the energy market provides another outlet for it.

A coal mine near Katowice in Silesia – the heart of Poland's mining region.

oland is particularly rich in natural resources. It also has a diverse and very active industrial sector, ranging from coal mining and shipbuilding to the new growth areas of tourism and financial services.

RESOURCES

COAL

Poland is among the world's eight largest producers of hard (black) and brown coal, and its output is exceeded only by much larger countries such as Russia, India, the United States and China. Reserves of hard coal in Poland are estimated at 45 billion tonnes, of which 30 to 50 percent are recoverable. Upper Silesia has 90 percent of these hard coal deposits. There are also an estimated 13 billion tonnes of brown coal, or lignite, and these are mainly located in the central regions. Nearly all of this brown coal is used to generate electricity.

OIL AND GAS

Poland has a long history of oil exploration and extraction. Ignacy Lukasiewicz drilled the world's first oil well in Bobrka, near Krosno, in 1854. Poland has estimated oil reserves of 96 million barrels (bbl), in 92 locations. (1 bbl = 159 liters.) The largest deposits, in lowland

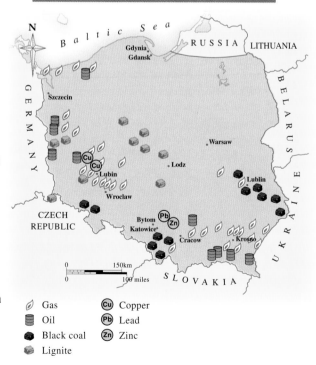

NATURAL RESOURCES

⌀ Gas	Cu Copper
▯ Oil	Pb Lead
◆ Black coal	Zn Zinc
◆ Lignite	

regions and beneath the Baltic Sea, make up more than 90 percent of the total, and there are smaller amounts in the Carpathian Mountains. One of the largest Baltic offshore oilfields produces around 1.9 million bbl of crude oil per year. Poland's total annual production of crude oil is estimated at 6.1 million bbl.

Natural gas reserves are estimated at 154 billion cubic meters, mainly in the Sudeten and Wielkopolskie lowlands and the Carpathian foothills. There are 242 gas fields in all, but not all of them are exploited.

A copper mine in Lubin, Lower Silesia, owned by Poland's largest producer.

METALS

Poland is one of the world's leading producers of copper. Large quantities are located in Lower Silesia, mostly in the Lubin region.

Polish resources of silver are estimated at 145,000 tonnes. Silver does not occur by itself in Poland, but is found together with copper ores or with lead and zinc. More than 90 percent of Polish silver is exported.

Lead-zinc ores are located in small quantities in the Silesia-Cracow region. These two metals have been exploited in Poland since the Middle Ages, and accessible resources now total around 7 million tonnes of zinc and 3 million tonnes of lead.

SULFUR

Sulfur is very important to the chemical industries, and there are huge deposits in Poland. However, less than 30 percent of Poland's sulfur is economically recoverable.

ROCK SALT

It is estimated that Poland's deposits of rock salt exceed 80 billion tonnes. The Wieliczka salt mine near Cracow has been in existence since the thirteenth century and is the world's oldest industrial enterprise in continuous operation.

AMBER

Amber is a transparent fossilized resin often associated with Poland, and it has been traded for centuries. Poland is still a major world supplier. The greatest concentrations are found around the Gulf of Gdansk on the Baltic coast.

TRADING PARTNERS (% OF VALUE), 2003

EXPORTS

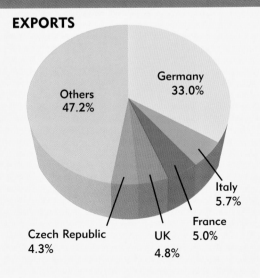

Others 47.2%
Germany 33.0%
Italy 5.7%
France 5.0%
UK 4.8%
Czech Republic 4.3%

IMPORTS

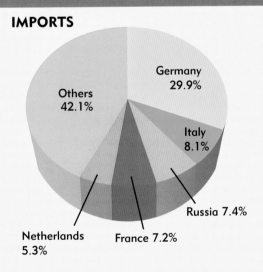

Others 42.1%
Germany 29.9%
Italy 8.1%
Russia 7.4%
France 7.2%
Netherlands 5.3%

Source: *CIA World Factbook*, 2004

MANUFACTURING INDUSTRY

STEELWORKS

A worker in the fierce heat of the steelworks in Katowice.

Before 1989, Poland's metals industry was closely tied to the defense industry, producing weapons for the Soviet bloc. After the breakup of the Warsaw Pact in 1991, both these sectors suffered setbacks. Poland needed to modernize them in order to reduce overemployment and increase productivity and quality. Today these industries are far more efficient and competitive in world markets. The largest steelworks – Huta Katowice, Nowa Huta and Huta Warszawa – have undergone radical changes, and many workers have lost their jobs. However, there has also been a significant reduction in pollution as a result of modernization.

MOTOR INDUSTRY

Poland has a long history of car manufacturing and has been making Fiat cars under licence since the 1930s. Today many of the world's leading car companies have factories in Poland. Fiat is still the largest foreign investor, and it has invested over US$1.5 billion since it started operations. General Motors also has a strong presence. Some foreign companies produce parts for their cars in Poland, and the construction of truck and bus bodies and chassis (frames) is an important part of the Polish industry. The car industry is the second-largest export sector in Poland.

SHIPBUILDING

Poland has been a world leader in shipbuilding for decades. The main shipyards are in Gdynia, Gdansk and Szczecin. The shipyard at Szczecin has built more than 600 ships in total. However, with the political changes of 1989, the shipyards suddenly lost most of their work from the Communist countries and quickly had to find new customers in Europe. There was a rush to modernize, and the early 1990s saw rapid growth. By 1996, though, both the Gdansk and Gdynia yards were in financial trouble.

Cars on the assembly line at the Daewoo car plant in Warsaw.

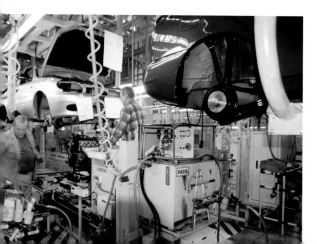

When Gdynia Shipyard Group took over the Gdansk Shipyard in 1997, the new owners decided not to continue with the business as it was because the sheer size of the site and the number of employees made it unlikely to succeed. So it sold 73 hectares of the shipyard to Synergia 99, a real estate development company. The company plans to transform the mostly run-down site into a new Gdansk district called Mlode Miasto (Young City). Roman Sebastyanski, Marketing Director of Synergia 99, says, "Our main aim is to reshape this district, to give it a new character. We want the local perception of this area to change from that of dead land." The plan is to make the district multifunctional, while keeping many of its historical elements. Stocznia Gdanska, the original owner, still rents space for shipbuilding, but now there are many other enterprises too.

Launching the hull of a trawler in the shipyard in Gdansk.

Sebastyanski also stresses the importance of Synergia's noncommercial activities, saying, "We want to make this area an inspiration for artists." In fact there is already an active artists' commune in a converted telephone exchange building, and the National Theater of Pomerania regularly performs plays in what was the main shipbuilding hall. Other plans for this huge site include a promenade of several kilometers along the waterfront, housing and offices, an entertainment complex, a marina and a hotel.

Fortunes picked up in 1996 when a new boss – Janusz Szlanta, an ex-banker – took over at Gdynia. Within a year the shipyard made profits of US$16 million, and Gdynia Shipyard Group bought the Gdansk Shipyard. Despite further problems for Gdynia in 2002, recent orders worth more than US$1,600 million will keep this shipyard busy until at least 2006. The industry expects that EU

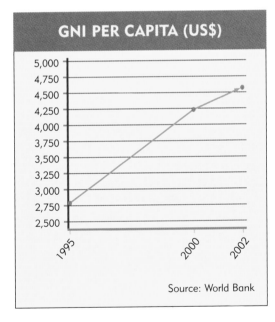

GNI PER CAPITA (US$)

Source: World Bank

ECONOMIC STRUCTURE, 2004 (% GDP CONTRIBUTIONS)

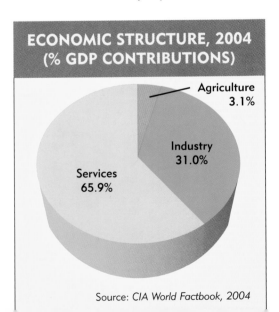

Agriculture 3.1%

Industry 31.0%

Services 65.9%

Source: CIA World Factbook, 2004

membership will boost business further. Poland already has around 17 percent of the market in Europe. The Polish industry will help the European Union to compete with China, Japan and South Korea in shipbuilding.

Workers at the Miraculum cosmetics factory in Cracow. Polish cosmetics production is increasing.

UNEMPLOYMENT RATE, 1990–2003 (AS % OF ECONOMICALLY ACTIVE POPULATION)

Source: GUS (Central Statistical Office, Poland)

TEXTILES

The textile industry is based mainly in the city of Lodz in central Poland. This sector has also been through difficult reforms since the end of Communism and has struggled to compete against cheap imported fabrics and clothes, particularly from Southeast Asia. However, recent figures suggest that the industry is beginning to stabilize and grow once more. Most Polish textile exports are sold to other EU countries.

CHEMICALS

The chemical industry is still in a process of change, but production is growing in some areas. Companies making basic chemical products, such as plastics, fertilizers and rubber, have seen marked growth in production. This looks likely to continue. The 1990s saw an increase in demand for PVC products for use in building, and the production of cosmetics is also growing. Foreign investors currently hold about 15 percent of shares in the largest chemicals firms in Poland, and state-owned companies make up only 0.5 percent of all companies in the industry.

COAL MINING

Coal is still the main energy source in Poland. The coal-mining industry is based in Upper Silesia, and the cities of Katowice, Bytom, Gliwice, Zabrze and Sosnowiec all grew up around the industry. Brown coal (lignite) is excavated from strip mines in central Poland, and 98 percent of this goes to fuel power stations.

Most of Poland's energy comes from brown coal extracted from strip mines like this one.

With mines closing, young men in Bytom will have to look elsewhere for work.

The city of Bytom in Upper Silesia has a population of 210,000. Two of the four Silesian coal mines chosen for closure in April 2004 were in Bytom – Bytom II and Centrum. This meant the loss of 8,600 mining jobs in a city where the unemployment rate was already around 20 percent. In 2003 there were large-scale demonstrations against these proposals and violent clashes between police and demonstrators in Warsaw. Many laid-off miners feel that they have little chance of other employment, and the city council of Bytom predicted that these mine closures would turn the city into a ghost town.

With the change to a free-market economy and a decline in the worldwide demand for coal, Poland has had to make its mining sector more competitive and efficient. The industry has undergone major restructuring since 1990, and this has been a difficult process. Under Communism there was enormous development of the industry, and miners enjoyed good pay and social status. During the 1980s, Poland was producing nearly 200 million tonnes of coal per year. By the 1990s, Poland's coal output was higher than its domestic demand, and other countries had cheaper suppliers elsewhere. Production was gradually cut to 100 million tonnes a year between 1990 and 2000. Current plans are to reduce this to 88 million tonnes by 2006.

Reforms from 1990 to the present have had some success, but there has been resistance from miners and their unions because restructuring has brought job losses. Since 1989 the workforce has been reduced from 450,000 workers to around 100,000 today, and a further cut of 36,000 is planned by 2006. Poland has closed 23 out of the 64 mines that were operating in the 1980s, with Upper Silesia most affected. Severance pay has been generous, though. The cost to the Polish state of mining reforms has been enormous – the total figure to 2001 is nearly US$10 billion – and the government is determined to cut this public spending. Assistance has come from the European Union and the World Bank.

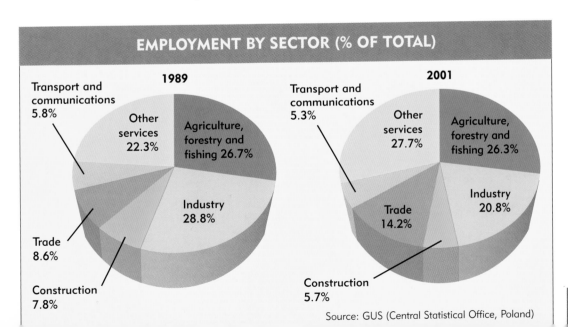

EMPLOYMENT BY SECTOR (% OF TOTAL)

1989

Transport and communications 5.8%

Other services 22.3%

Agriculture, forestry and fishing 26.7%

Industry 28.8%

Trade 8.6%

Construction 7.8%

2001

Transport and communications 5.3%

Other services 27.7%

Agriculture, forestry and fishing 26.3%

Industry 20.8%

Trade 14.2%

Construction 5.7%

Source: GUS (Central Statistical Office, Poland)

SERVICE INDUSTRIES

As the heavy industry and manufacturing sectors have undergone tough reforms to make them more efficient, their share in the economy has fallen. In the service sector the picture is reversed, and there has been great expansion. This sector now accounts for more than 60 percent of Poland's GDP.

The changes in the economy and government policy have brought an increase in trade and tourism and a boom in the telecommunications and information technology (IT) industries. The government has also strongly promoted business activities by small and medium-sized enterprises. In 1999 these made up 99.76 percent of all registered companies in Poland. Polish policy has encouraged their growth by reducing the complicated bureaucracy involved in setting up and running businesses.

FINANCIAL SERVICES AND ADVERTISING

Under Communism, the financial services industry was practically nonexistent. Now it is extremely active and is developing fast. This sector includes areas such as insurance and banking, and it attracts a lot of foreign investment. In 2003, 30 percent of all foreign direct investment in Poland went into the financial services sector – 12 percent more than in 2002.

There has also been rapid growth in the advertising and promotion industries, and these are now very similar to those found anywhere else in Europe.

Surf, work, play – there are now many Internet cafés in Poland.

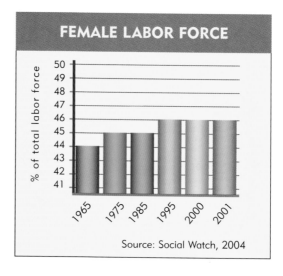

Source: Social Watch, 2004

INFORMATION TECHNOLOGY

The Polish IT market is developing rapidly, and major international companies such as Microsoft, Hewlett-Packard, IBM and Oracle are all present in the country along with Polish firms such as Prokom, ComputerLand and ComArch. The total value of the market is now around € 16 billion (US$20.8 billion), excluding telecommunications services. This is expected to increase by nearly 10 percent in 2005. Growth in this sector is now the largest in the whole economy.

Today 2 million to 3 million Poles have Internet access, and access is expanding. There are also many Internet cafés in Polish cities.

Stockbrokers at work at the Warsaw Stock Exchange.

PERSONAL COMPUTERS

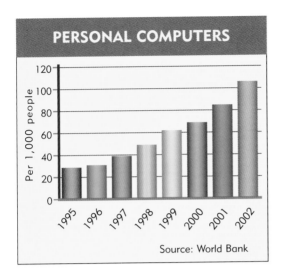

Per 1,000 people

Source: World Bank

TELECOMMUNICATIONS DATA (PER 1,000 PEOPLE)

Mainline phones	295
Mobile phones	363
Internet users	230

Source: World Bank

TELEVISION SETS

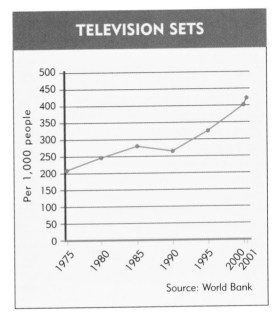

Per 1,000 people

Source: World Bank

TELECOMMUNICATIONS

The main telecommunications provider in Poland is Telekomunikacja Polska SA, or TPSA. This was a state monopoly until 2002, when the market for long-distance service was opened up to other firms. International service followed in 2003. In 2001 TPSA was rated the largest company in Central and Eastern Europe, and it has more than 90 percent of the Polish market in mainline telephones. The cost of using such telephones in Poland is quite high compared with other countries. As a result, far more Poles have mobile phones than mainline phones. Around 13.5 million Poles have cell phones, and the number of cell phones in use is growing by 30 percent every year.

Mobile phones are a part of everyday life in Poland.

Krupowki Street, the main street in Zakopane, is packed with tourists in winter and summer.

TOURISM

Poland has become a very attractive destination for tourists in recent years. There are many historical sites and natural attractions to visit, and tourism is an expanding sector of the Polish economy. The numbers of visitors rose sharply during the 1990s, peaking in 1997 at around 19 million for that year. The Polish government wants to develop the industry as much as possible, and in 2001 it approved a tourism development strategy to support and promote small and medium-sized tourism businesses. Tourism will certainly be helped by EU membership and by new low-fare airlines offering service to Poland. At present, the majority of tourists to Poland come from Germany.

Over the past 15 years there has been a vast improvement in the number and quality of hotels, guest houses and other types of accommodations for tourists. Even in very remote rural areas there are many small *pensjonaty* (inns) offering rooms for visitors. Traveling around within Poland is becoming more expensive than it used to be, but it is still cheaper than travel in Western Europe. Eating out and tickets for exhibitions and concerts are also very reasonably priced. Poland is a very safe country to travel in, and Polish people are genuinely hospitable and friendly toward strangers.

CULTURAL AND HISTORICAL TOURISM

Many tourists are attracted to Poland because of its unique and eventful history. Traces of the country's past can be seen in every city and every different region. The Piast and Jagiellon dynasties, the rule of the Teutonic Knights, the trade of the Hanseatic League, the battlegrounds of World War II and atrocities of the Holocaust, rule by Soviet Communism and the wave of political change in the 1980s have all left behind buildings, artifacts and symbolic remnants that can be seen today.

Cracow, Warsaw, Gdansk and Wroclaw are centers for this kind of historical tourism, as well as for their offerings of Polish art, music and theater.

Other tourist sites include the Wieliczka salt mines near Cracow, which are now a museum, and Jasna Gora near Czestochowa, one of the most important Catholic pilgrimage sites in Europe because of its famous painting of the Black Madonna. Zakopane, a mountain town at the foot of the Tatras, is another place of cultural interest to foreigners. Here the customs, art and architecture of the Gorale (mountain people) draw large numbers of tourists every year.

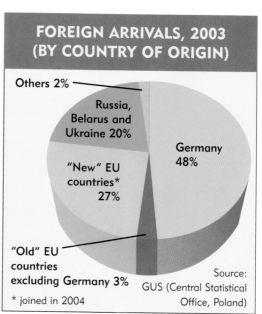

FOREIGN ARRIVALS, 2003 (BY COUNTRY OF ORIGIN)

Others 2%

Russia, Belarus and Ukraine 20%

"New" EU countries* 27%

Germany 48%

"Old" EU countries excluding Germany 3%

* joined in 2004

Source: GUS (Central Statistical Office, Poland)

Poland has many areas that are rich in mineral waters, and some of these are now popular health resorts. Different springs are thought to have different health benefits. For example, the water at Polanica Zdroj in Lower Silesia is supposed to be good for the circulation and digestive system disorders. Rabka Zdroj, in the Podhale region of Malopolskie, is called "The Children of the World's Town" and is the main health resort in Poland specializing in helping children. The town combines a wide range of health services with many sports and leisure facilities. Local hospitals specialize in treating rheumatism, allergies, diabetes and breathing

A therapist leads some pool exercises at Polanica Zdroj.

problems, among other conditions. There are also ski runs, horse-riding centers, tennis courts and an ice rink in Rabka.

The fourteenth-century Niedzica Castle, which once marked Poland's border with Hungary, looks out across the Dunajec River.

The Tatra Mountains are a popular destination for climbers — there is no shortage of this kind of rugged terrain.

NATURAL ATTRACTIONS

Poland offers a wide range of options to tourists interested in the natural world and outdoor pursuits. Beach vacations on the Baltic have been popular among Poles and Germans for a long time, and now more foreign visitors are discovering Poland's northern beach resorts. Other options include vacation cottages along the Mazurian lakes, bird-watching tours in the forests, and wildlife-spotting trips in the national parks.

Activity vacations are also becoming popular among foreign visitors. These include long-distance bicycle tours, climbing in the Tatras, sailing and canoeing on the northern lakes, and even paragliding in the mountains. In season there are good opportunities for skiing and other winter sports in the south.

AGROTOURISM

Agrotourism has recently expanded as a part of the tourism market, and around 11,000 Polish farms are now providing this type of vacation. Visitors are offered housing on a farm and meals that are usually produced entirely locally. In most cases they can join in the farm activities and enjoy rural pursuits, such as horseback-riding and fishing. Agrotourism is getting strong support from the Polish state, in its effort to promote small businesses and diversify activities in rural areas.

LEFT: Visitors meet the animals at a farm offering agrotourism.

CASE STUDY
A SMALL POLISH FARM

The Kobiela family farms just over 6 hectares of land near Zawoja in the Beskid Mountains. Franciszek Kobiela inherited the farm from his parents in the mid-1970s. At that time the farm produced and sold meat, eggs, dairy products and linen, among other things. Thirty years ago Franciszek's wife Helena started to rent out one room to guests as a way of increasing the low profits from farming. Today they can accommodate 25 people on their certified organic farm, which is managed jointly by Franciszek, Helena and two of their adult children, Katarzyna and Grzegorz. All their produce is now consumed on the farm. The land is mostly pasture, though they grow some potatoes, rye, wheat, oats and vegetables. They keep two cows, two bulls, two pigs, some rabbits and chickens, and a horse. Most of the work on the farm is done manually or with the horse, because the terrain is hilly. They have machines for cutting and turning hay, harrowing soil, plowing, and digging up potatoes. The Kobielas take in tourists all year round, both from Poland and abroad. Most of their guests are families with children, retired people, and schoolchildren on

Agrotourism has a lot to offer families with young children.

organized trips. Katarzyna and Grzegorz, who now legally own the farm, have completed studies to help them in managing the enterprise – Katarzyna in marketing and management, and Grzegorz in tourism services. They have also trained in specific aspects of agrotourism, and Grzegorz is a qualified guide to the Beskid Mountains. Both of them have learned English and German to help in attracting foreign tourists to their farm.

TRANSPORT, ENERGY AND THE ENVIRONMENT

A PKP train pulls into Warsaw Central Station.

Poland is continually modernizing its transport and energy sectors. Both of these have an impact on the natural environment, and great efforts are being made to protect the environment from the potentially harmful effects of economic development. Since 1990 efforts to reduce pollution levels have been highly successful.

TRANSPORT

TRANSPORT (map)

- Main road
- ++++ Railway
- ✈ International airport

0 ————— 150km
0 ————— 100 miles

Baltic Sea

RUSSIA   LITHUANIA

Darłowo   Gdynia   Gdańsk
Szczecin
GERMANY
Bydgoszcz   Białystok
Poznan
Warsaw   Siedlce
Pruszkow
Lodz   BELARUS
Legnica   Wroclaw   Lublin
Kielce
CZECH REPUBLIC   Bytom   Cracow
Katowice   UKRAINE
Zagorze

TRANSPORT
AIR

Poland has international airports in Warsaw, Cracow and Gdansk. Warsaw Frederic Chopin Airport has flights to most major European cities, as well as further afield. In 2004 building began on a new second terminal, and by 2005 the airport should be able to handle 10 million passengers a year. The original terminal was designed for 3.5 million but already handles 5 million people every year. Gdansk also built a new passenger terminal for its Rebiechowo airport, completed in 1997. Rebiechowo was renamed Lech Walesa Airport in 2004 to mark the airport's thirtieth anniversary. Developments are also under way at regional airports, including Katowice, Szczecin and Poznan.

Trams (streetcars) are a feature of all major Polish cities. Combined with buses they form a reliable public transportation network. Trams run on electricity from overhead cables, and because they do not emit direct exhaust fumes they are friendly to the local environment. Warsaw has a total of 122km of tram lines, with 32 different routes. Of these, 29 routes operate all day, seven days a week. An estimated 1.5 million passengers use the Warsaw tram and bus network every day, compared with 100,000 using the subway.

A tram on a busy route through the center of Warsaw.

RAIL

International rail links connect Warsaw with many European cities, including Berlin, Budapest, St Petersburg, Moscow, Paris, Prague and Vienna. There are also lines from Berlin to Gdansk and Cologne to Cracow. The state-owned railway company, Polskie Koleje Panstwowe (PKP), was split into several companies in 2001. Together the PKP branches have more than 22,000km of lines in Poland.

Warsaw has an underground rail system, or subway, which was opened in 1995. It has 15 stations on one line; two more lines are planned for contruction.

ROAD

Poland's roads are in a generally poor state, and extensive modernization is needed. Though Poland has important international road connections, it has no modern highway network. Eight international road routes meet in Warsaw, including the A2 from Berlin to Moscow, but there is no highway circling the capital city. It is estimated that PLN 1.2 billion (US$380 million) will be required every year just to keep Poland's roads in their current condition. Poland received a loan of €100 million (US$130 million) from the World Bank in 2004 for road maintenance work, and EU funds will provide a further €17.5 billion (US$23 billion) for the construction of new roads through 2015.

The number of vehicles on Polish roads is growing rapidly. Cars are increasing by 7 percent a year and heavy trucks by 11 percent. In the cities, buses are the most common form of public transportation. The Polish bus company PKS also runs service between cities, and these are usually cheaper than the trains.

SEA

There are sea freight lines going to and from the northern ports of Szczecin-Swinoujscie, Gdansk and Gdynia. The port complex at Szczecin can handle up to 20 million tonnes of cargo a year. Passenger ferries also sail from these ports to Sweden and Denmark.

The ferry waits in port at Gdansk to take passengers to Sweden.

ENERGY
ENERGY POLICY

The main aim of Poland's energy policy is to ensure that there is enough fuel and energy for its own needs, and for other EU members. In order to achieve this, the Polish government is broadening the range of its energy supplies and taking steps to improve efficiency and protect the environment. As a new EU member, Poland has the opportunity to implement the most modern energy programs, drawing on the experience of other countries.

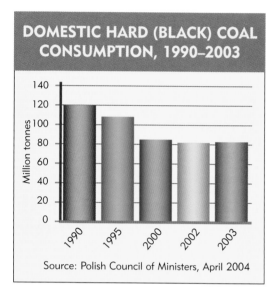

DOMESTIC HARD (BLACK) COAL CONSUMPTION, 1990–2003

Source: Polish Council of Ministers, April 2004

ELECTRICITY BALANCE, 2001 (BILLION kWh)

Electricity production	135.0
Electricity consumption	118.8
Electricity exports	11.0
Electricity imports	4.3

Source: CIA World Factbook, 2004

COAL

Some 97 percent of Poland's energy comes from coal-fired power stations, though this proportion is falling. Much of the fuel used in these plants is brown coal (lignite), and most power stations have been built close to mines. The largest coal-fired power station in the country – and in Europe – is at Belchatow in central Poland. Brown coal was discovered here in the 1960s, and the power station has been producing electricity since 1981. It provides more than 20 percent of Poland's domestic electricity supply.

NUCLEAR POWER

Poland has no nuclear power stations. In the 1970s there were plans to build three, and work began on a plant in Zarnowiec, near Gdansk, in 1974. After much discussion and public opposition – particularly after the 1986 Chernobyl reactor accident in the Soviet Union – the plans were abandoned in 1990. There are no current plans to build any nuclear plants until at least 2015, but because the EU has a general commitment to developing nuclear energy, this may change.

A coal-fired power station on the bank of the Vistula River in Warsaw.

OIL

Poland does not have enough oil reserves to meet its needs and imports oil from the Middle East, Norway, the United Kingdom and North Africa. The rest comes from Russia by pipeline. The northern port of Gdansk was extensively rebuilt in 1992 to provide access for oil tankers.

HYDROELECTRIC POWER

Hydroelectric power (HEP) provides only 1 to 2 percent of Poland's energy. The largest HEP station is on the Dunajec River at Niedzica. This is used for power production during times of peak demand. There is also a system of dams with power stations on the Sola River (a tributary of the Vistula).

Welders completing the first section of the gas pipeline from Russia to Poland.

NATURAL GAS

As coal declines as an energy source, the use of natural gas is expected to increase. It is estimated that the share of gas in power generation in Poland could rise by 40 percent between 2000 and 2025.

Poland imports most of its natural gas from Russia. In 1990 and 1991 there was much exploration of Poland's own resources, and the country was declared potentially self-sufficient. Poland has made efforts to reduce its reliance on Russian gas and to broaden its sources of supply. It has signed gas supply agreements with Germany and Norway.

CASE STUDY
NIEDZICA HEP STATION

Plans for a dam and hydroelectric power station at Niedzica started as early as 1905. The power station began operating in 1997, despite opposition from local and environmental groups. The dam wall is 550m long, and the reservoir covers 1,147km^2 and holds around 230 million m^3 of water. This reservoir proved very useful for flood protection in 1997: At its peak on 9 July the river water was entering the reservoir at seven times the usual flow rate. Storage in the reservoir protected areas downstream of the dam.

The view down the river from the dam wall at Niedzica HEP station.

Turbines catch the wind on the Baltic coast near Darlowo.

ELECTRICITY SUPPLY

The Polish electricity supply system is operated by Polskie Sieci Elektroenergetyczne (PSE). PSE is responsible for the transmission of electrical power around the country and maintenance of the system. It also buys electricity from other suppliers and sells it to regional utility companies and industrial customers. The Polish electricity system is now connected to the power transmission grid in Western Europe, which allows Poland to sell surplus power to other countries. This also makes Poland's electricity supply more secure, since it can buy power if it needs to. Poland has also maintained its links with the Ukrainian and Belarusian grid systems.

ELECTRICITY PRODUCTION BY SOURCE, 2001

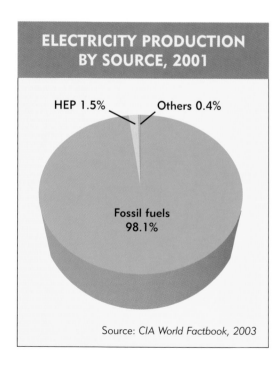

HEP 1.5%   Others 0.4%

Fossil fuels
98.1%

Source: *CIA World Factbook, 2003*

EU LAWS AND THE ENVIRONMENT

The European Union places great importance on protecting the environment, and Poland is no exception. Like other countries, Poland has to balance its increasing energy needs against potential pollution and environmental damage. The first Polish law relating to protection of the environment in energy production was passed in 1997. It has led to the modernization of coal-fired power stations and reduced polluting emissions. Poland is also committed to greater use of renewable energy sources such as wind power, biogas and geothermal energy.

RENEWABLE ENERGY

In 1999 Poland's parliament passed resolutions requiring the country to make greater use of its renewable energy sources. In 2000 the government announced its goal to raise the share of energy production provided by renewable sources to 7.5 percent by 2010, and to 15 percent by 2020.

Poland has reasonably good renewable energy resources. Apart from large-scale HEP plants like the one at Niedzica, there are many sites suitable for small-scale installations on rivers. Several wind farms are already operating. The first of these was commissioned in 1999, near Darlowo on the Baltic coast. By 2000 there were 22 wind farms (some of which were only single turbines) connected to the Polish grid. The largest wind farm in Poland, the Zagorze Wind Power Plant, with 15 wind turbines, began operating in April 2003.

Poland has several areas where geothermal energy can be exploited, and other types of renewable energy use are being developed. Two examples are biogas – using gas from waste dumps to generate power – and the use of wood from sustainable forests as a power source.

Renewable energy use greatly increased during the late 1990s, following the passage of a law in 1997 obliging all Polish power distribution companies to include renewable sources in their future plans. Current EU law also requires energy companies to obtain a minimum of 2.4 percent of all the energy they sell from renewable sources. This figure is set to rise in the future.

CASE STUDY
BREC

The Baltic Renewable Energy Centre (BREC) was founded in 1994 by the European Commission. It is responsible for carrying out state policy on renewable energy. There are two BREC offices, one in Warsaw and one in Gdansk. Experts from BREC work on various renewable energy projects throughout Poland, and the center also works with other institutions within the EU. As well as research and development work, BREC plays a role in public information and education about renewable energy issues.

Staff at the Baltic Renewable Energy Centre in Gdansk.

THE ENVIRONMENT

During Communist times, the drive toward heavy industrialization in Poland ignored any effects on the natural environment. The results of this were high levels of water and air pollution and, in some areas, catastrophic environmental damage.

Since 1990 the field of environmental protection and conservation has changed dramatically. There has been marked success in some areas and less in others, but overall Poland is committed to improving the state of the environment. Currently around 2 percent of GDP is allocated to this purpose. The top priorities are pollution prevention, waste management, wastewater treatment, and protecting biodiversity (the range of different forms of life).

AIR POLLUTION

The region worst affected by the heavy industrialization of the Communist era was Upper Silesia, the heartland of the mining and steel industries. In the 1980s, Katowice produced up to 25 percent of Poland's total emissions of sulfur dioxide (SO_2) and nitrogen

Children playing near a factory with high pollutant emissions in Silesia.

oxides (NOx). Sulfur dioxide emissions from Upper Silesia at this time amounted to around 3 million tons a year. This region, where Poland's borders met East Germany and Czechoslovakia, was known as "The Black Triangle" because of the amount of pollution in the air.

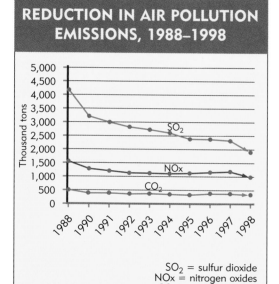

REDUCTION IN AIR POLLUTION EMISSIONS, 1988–1998

SO_2 = sulfur dioxide
NOx = nitrogen oxides
CO_2 = carbon dioxide

Source: Polish Ministry of the Environment

A municipal waste dump at Lubna, outside Warsaw.

However, airborne industrial pollution has been cut by more than 50 percent since the 1980s. The reduction in SO_2 emissions over this period is estimated at 53 percent. This improvement has come as a result of new laws, the modernization of industries, and investment in cleaner technology. There is still much work to be done to improve air quality, particularly regarding vehicle exhausts. Road traffic in Poland has doubled in the past 10 years, raising pollution levels.

WASTE MANAGEMENT

In 1997, Poland produced around 30 million tonnes of waste – nearly one tonne per person. As the quantity of consumer goods has increased in the new economy, the amount of waste has risen too, and disposing of it is now a major problem. At present, more than 90 percent of solid waste is buried in landfill sites, and the amount of waste in them has doubled in the last 15 years. Around a third of existing landfill capacity is already full. There are not many municipal waste incinerators in Poland. Other options for waste disposal include recycling, composting and using waste as an energy source.

CASE STUDY
NOWA HUTA

The Lenin Steelworks at Nowa Huta, just outside Cracow, was one of the worst polluters in Communist Poland. The industrial and residential complex of Nowa Huta was built in 1949 as a model of socialist planning. By the mid-1960s its steel mill was the largest in Europe. In the late 1970s, it employed almost 40,000 people and produced nearly 7 million tonnes of steel a year. Air pollution from Nowa Huta's chimneys was very heavy up until the end of the 1980s, when it was emitting into the atmosphere an estimated 170 tonnes of lead, 470 tonnes of zinc and 7 tonnes of cadmium every year. The economic changes of 1990 brought about a major drop in steel production, and the emissions level decreased. Modernization has also greatly reduced the pollution from the plant. The steelworks has been renamed Huta Sendzimira.

The renamed steelworks – a monumental sign for a monumental enterprise.

WATER POLLUTION

The two main sources of water pollution are inadequately treated wastewater from towns and cities, and industrial pollution. The amounts of both these sources have decreased considerably since the beginning of the 1990s, thanks to modernization of industry, better use of water in households, and the construction of many new water-treatment plants. National policy is focused on the construction of more such plants and the modernization of existing systems.

RIVERS

During the 1970s and 1980s, Poland's rivers were heavily polluted. Much of this pollution came from the waste products of heavy industry. The worst cases were the Vistula and Oder Rivers, partly because of the large number of industrial sites in the southern and southwestern regions of Poland. These regions are in the upper parts of the Vistula and Oder river basins, so pollutants that enter the rivers there affect the river along its entire length.

Warsaw also accounted for a large proportion of wastewater entering the Vistula. A 1992 report identified 3,614 areas in Poland

Visible pollution of the Oder River. Fortunately such sights are becoming much less common.

that were contributing to Baltic Sea pollution via the rivers. Between this time and 2000, Poland carried out a number of successful actions to reduce this figure, and many of the worst-polluted spots have been cleaned up.

The Oder River flows in the territory of different countries, so joint action is necessary to keep it clean. It is under the authority of the International Commission for the Protection of the Oder River Against Pollution, which was founded in 1996 as a joint program of Poland, Germany, the Czech Republic and the European Union. Poland has other water agreements with Slovakia, Belarus and Ukraine.

EFFECTS OF AGRICULTURE

Pollutants entering groundwater – water held in the soil and rock – from agriculture are currently not a large problem. However, there are concerns that an increase in large-scale and more intensive farming methods may produce more groundwater pollution. Some animal farming methods produce huge quantities of waste, which has to be treated properly in order to be environmentally safe. There are also questions about the possible effects of intensive farming methods on Polish wildlife. In other countries changes in farming have reduced the numbers of several species of birds on farmland, and this may also occur in Poland.

FORESTS

More than 28 percent of Poland's total area is covered by forest. Drought, forest fires and insect attack are three major natural threats to these areas. Insect attack in particular has increased since the 1970s because of changes in the climate. One particular example of serious insect damage to trees can be seen in the Karkonosze Mountains. Pollution of the air and water caused by human activities are the most serious threats to the forests, however. The greatest danger is from high levels of sulfur dioxide and nitrogen oxides in the air. This results in acid rain, which causes great damage to trees. Once again, the areas that have been most affected by airborne pollution are found in the "Black Triangle" in southwestern Poland, and particularly in the western Sudeten Mountains.

Trees killed by acid rain in the Karkonosze Mountains, Lower Silesia.

Around 16 percent of Poland's forest is privately owned, and some of this is of low quality because of poor management. Forests owned and managed by the state are generally in much better condition.

Airborne pollution from coal-burning leaves its mark at street level in Katowice.

This part of the Praga district in Warsaw is destined for urban renewal.

U rban life in Poland is as diverse and varied as its individual cities, and even as the inhabitants themselves. There are distinctive characteristics of Polish cities, though, and also many important changes taking place in the urban areas of Poland.

URBANIZATION

Currently 62 percent of the Polish population live in urban areas, and this is increasing at a rate of nearly 2 percent a year. Of that 62 percent, about 15 percent live in Warsaw. The reasons for the continuing movement toward the cities are mostly economic – people are moving to find more work and enjoy a better standard of living. The economic changes that have taken place in Poland since 1989 have made the cities more attractive to growing numbers of people. However, increasing urbanization requires more housing and improved infrastructure – buildings, roads and communications networks. It also raises uncertainties regarding Polish rural areas. The economic gap between urban and rural regions in Poland is widening, making it difficult for people in the countryside to move to the cities because of the cost. In spite of this Poland's cities are expected to keep on growing.

DECLINE AND URBAN RENEWAL

In Poland, as in most other countries, there are parts of cities that have fallen into decline. Ageing buildings, housing that needs major repairs and vacant industrial land (or "brownfield" sites) are a major issue for Poland. Attempts to revitalize run-down city districts started at the beginning of the 1990s, but many such projects failed to reach completion. Key problems have been underfinancing and the inexperience of project managers in coordinating such large urban renewal developments. There have been some notable successes, however, such as in the Praga district of Warsaw and the Manufaktura project in Lodz. The Manufaktura scheme turned a large, disused factory area in Lodz into a shopping and entertainment center.

Apart from rebuilding in declining areas, there is a great deal of new housing and commercial construction springing up all across Poland. Warsaw is one of the fastest-

URBAN POPULATION

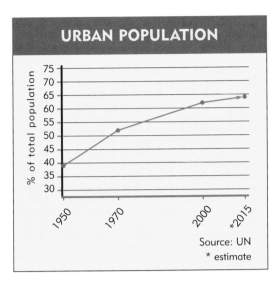

Source: UN
* estimate

Major commercial building work under way near the Palac Kultury in the center of Warsaw.

growing cities in Europe, with new offices, apartment buildings and shopping centers being built all the time. Since 1999 the value of new construction in the city has reached more than US$5 billion. Polish architects are being very innovative and lively in the design of new buildings. The trend for high-rise towers has passed, and the use of bright colors and modern, nontraditional forms of building is on the increase. These new commercial and housing developments are signs of Poland's rapidly expanding economy.

A new business center on the outskirts of Warsaw ready for occupants.

POLAND'S CITIES

Each of Poland's major cities has a distinctive character. Their histories, and the influences on them, have been quite different. For example, Cracow was the capital until 1596, and escaped destruction in World War II. This makes it very different from Warsaw, which rose to importance later and was then virtually destroyed by 1945.

The port cities of Gdansk and Gdynia, the commercial centers of Poznan and Lodz, and the industrial base of Katowice all show different aspects of urban life in Poland.

A Polish woman shows her European Community passport.

The twentieth century was a time of great difficulties and frequent change for the Polish people. National independence lasted only for the years between the two World Wars, and democracy then emerged again for the last decade of the century. Now that Poland is once more a strong and thriving country, it faces a new set of challenges and opportunities.

NATO

In 1999 Poland joined the North Atlantic Treaty Organization (NATO), a mutual defense alliance among 26 countries including the United Kingdom and the United States. This step changed Poland's position in the world. Up until 1991, Poland was a member of the Warsaw Pact, a defense agreement among members of the old Soviet bloc. NATO membership means that Poland now has an important role to play in European military defense. On the global scale, Poland sent military forces to Iraq during the second Gulf War in 2003. Poland seems certain to have more involvement in military and peacekeeping operations around the world in the future.

EU MEMBERSHIP

Joining the European Union on 1 May 2004 brought Poland the chance to exert much more influence in European politics. Poland now has its own MEPs (members of the European Parliament) and full access to EU funding in many different sectors. European trade links are stronger and Poles can now live and work in other EU countries if they wish. In 2003 the majority of Poles voted in favor of joining the European Union. However, many of the older generation in Poland are unsure of what this change might bring. They have already experienced so much political change during their lives that they are not excited by the idea of more. The younger generation is already more Western in outlook than the previous one, and many younger Poles are becoming used to a lifestyle similar to that in other European countries.

One of the challenges that EU membership has brought to Poland is that of the change in borders. Before 2004 the edge of the European Union was between Germany and Poland. Now it is between Poland and its eastern neighbors, Belarus and Ukraine. This means that Poland is responsible for making these borders secure for its EU partners. This has already involved much investment and assistance from other EU countries.

Poland is a country with an enormous amount to offer. Its economy is growing stronger all the time, and it has great resources and a highly educated workforce. Some commentators say that it is a mistake to think only in terms of Poland becoming more Westernized, because they believe Poland will, in return, influence its Western neighbors.

The European Union's new eastern border, between Poland and Ukraine. This is the crossing at Kroscienko.

THE EU

ICELAND

● EU members

NORWAY
SWEDEN
FINLAND
ESTONIA
LATVIA
DENMARK
LITHUANIA
RUSSIA
R U S S I A
IRELAND
UNITED KINGDOM
BELARUS
NETHERLANDS
BELGIUM
GERMANY
POLAND
LUXEMBOURG
CZECH REPUBLIC
UKRAINE
SLOVAKIA
FRANCE
AUSTRIA
HUNGARY
MOLDOVA
SWITZERLAND
SLOVENIA
CROATIA
ROMANIA
GEORGIA
SAN MARINO
BOSNIA HERZEGOVINA
PORTUGAL
ANDORRA
MONACO
ITALY
YUGOSLAVIA
BULGARIA
ARMENIA
SPAIN
MACEDONIA
ALBANIA
T U R K E Y
GREECE
SYRIA
MOROCCO
ALGERIA
TUNISIA
MALTA
CYPRUS
LEBANON
IRAQ

Amber A fossilized resin of coniferous trees, used to make jewelry and ornaments. Transparent and yellow to reddish in color, it sometimes contains preserved insects trapped inside.

Arable farming Farming of crops such as wheat and vegetables.

Brownfield site An area of land that has been heavily polluted by industrial use and then abandoned.

CAP The Common Agricultural Policy of the European Union (EU). It is the system that provides regulations, advice and financial support for farmers in the countries within the EU.

Chassis The frame on which the body of a vehicle is built.

Collectivization The process, used by communist governments, of joining small farms together to make larger ones owned by the state.

Consumer goods Any items that are bought by the public.

Diversify To broaden an activity by extending the number of things involved.

Ethnicity The racial, national and tribal origins of a group of people.

EU (European Union) The group of European countries that have joined together to achieve closer political, social, economic and environmental cooperation. Ten new countries, including Poland, joined on 1 May 2004, bringing the total to 25. Its currency is the euro (€).

Free-market economy An economy that is open to the flow of goods and services, and is not centrally controlled.

GDP (Gross Domestic Product) A measure of national income. It is the value of all the goods and services produced within a country over a stated period (usually one year), charged at market prices and including taxes and subsidies.

Geothermal Relating to heat occurring naturally underground.

Gmina The smallest type of administrative region in Poland; a municipality.

GNI (Gross National Income) The monetary value of goods and services produced by a country plus any earnings from overseas in a single year. It used to be called Gross National Product (GNP).

Groundwater Water that is held in the soil and rock.

HEP (hydroelectric power) Electricity generated by water as it passes through turbines.

Infrastructure Systems of transport, communications and services (such as water, electricity, sewerage) that support an economy and society.

Intensive farming A farming system that concentrates resources, such as labor and fertilizer, over a relatively small land area to increase production.

Landfill site An area where municipal waste is buried.

Humidity The concentration of water vapor in the air.

Hypermarket A very large store that is a combination of a supermarket and a department store.

Maritime Relating to the sea.

Martial law Law that allows rule by the army, usually when there has been fighting against the government.

NATO (North Atlantic Treaty Organization) A mutual defense alliance between 26 countries, including the United States and many European nations.

Population structure The numbers and proportion of people in particular age groups within a population.

Renewable energy Any form of energy production using a source that will not run out, such as sun, wind or wave power.

Subsidy A contribution of money, especially by a government or institution to support a project.

Temperate Not having extremes of cold or heat.

Tributary A stream or river that flows into the main channel of a river.

Urbanization The increase and expansion of town and city areas.

Urban Renewal The process of reviving a poor city neighborhood by large-scale projects to build new or renovate existing housing.

Warsaw Pact A military defense alliance of the former Soviet-bloc countries (the Soviet Union, Bulgaria, Czechoslovakia, Hungary, Poland, Albania, East Germany and Romania), signed in Warsaw in 1955.

Wind farm An energy plant that uses wind turbines to produce electricity.

Wojewodztwo The largest type of administrative region in Poland. There are 16 *wojewodztwa* in Poland.

BOOKS TO READ:

GUIDEBOOKS:

Czerniewicz-Umer, Teresa, Malgorzata Omilanowska, and Jerzy S. Majewski. *Eyewitness Travel Guides: Poland*. Rev. ed. New York: Dorling Kindersley, 2003. Includes good coverage of Warsaw, Cracow, and the northern and eastern regions of Poland.

Dydynski, Krzysztof. *Lonely Planet Guide: Poland*. 4th ed. London: Lonely Planet Publications, 2002. A thorough and up-to-date guide to Poland, with illustrations and color photographs.

Salter, Mark. *The Rough Guide to Poland*. 5th ed. London: Rough Guides, 2002. A reliable and thorough guidebook.

HISTORY AND OTHER BOOKS:

Burke, Patrick. *Revolution in Europe, 1989*. New York: Thomson Learning, 1995. Examines the changes surrounding the fall of Communism in Central and Eastern Europe.

Craig, Mary. *Lech Walesa: The Leader of Solidarity and Campaigner for Freedom and Human Rights in Poland*. Milwaukee: Gareth Stevens Childen's Books, 1990. A look at the shipyard electrician who led Solidarity and became president of Poland and a Nobel Peace Prize winner.

Davies, Norman. *Heart of Europe: A Short History of Poland*. Oxford: Oxford University Press, 2001. A history of Poland, beginning in 1945.

Everett, Charles, and Barbara Everett. *The Changing Face of Poland*. Chicago: Raintree, 2004. Presents information on the geography and climate, history, natural resources, economy, customs, and people of Poland, focusing on change in recent years.

Lukowski, Jerzy, and Hubert Zawadzki. *A Concise History of Poland*. Cambridge: Cambridge University Press, 2001. An introduction to Polish history, from medieval times to the present.

Malam, John. *Hitler Invades Poland: September 1, 1939*. North Mankato, Minn.: Smart Apple Media, 2003. A book exploring what happened on this historic day, with background information, photographs, and maps.

Otfinoski, Steven. *Nations in Transition: Poland*. New York: Facts On File, Inc., 2004. An excellent introduction to Poland, both for general-interest reading and for school reports.

Szulc, Tad. "Poland: The Hope That Never Dies." *National Geographic* 173, no.1 (1988): 80–121. A long and detailed article about Poland, written just before the political events of 1989.

Zamoyski, Adam. *The Polish Way: A Thousand-Year History of the Poles and Their Culture*. New York: Hippocrene Books, 1993. An introduction to Polish history.

WEBSITES:

The CIA World Factbook
http://www.cia.gov/cia/publications/factbook/geos/pl.html
The US Central Intelligence Agency's online factbook, with statistics and assessments of all countries of the world.

Poland.pl
http://www.poland.pl
Poland's official website for news and information.

Adminet Poland
http://www.admi.net/world/pl
Links to a variety of information about Poland.

The Official Website of the City of Warsaw
http://www.e-warsaw.pl/index.php
News and information about the capital city of Poland.

Central Statistical Office (GUS)
http://www.stat.gov.pl/english/index.htm
The official Polish government website for statistics about Poland.

METRIC CONVERSION TABLE

To convert	to	do this
mm (millimeters)	inches	divide by 25.4
cm (centimeters)	inches	divide by 2.54
m (meters)	feet	multiply by 3.281
m (meters)	yards	multiply by 1.094
km (kilometers)	yards	multiply by 1094
km (kilometers)	miles	divide by 1.6093
kilometers per hour	miles per hour	divide by 1.6093
cm^2 (square centimeters)	square inches	divide by 6.452
m^2 (square meters)	square feet	multiply by 10.76
m^2 (square meters)	square yards	multiply by 1.196
km^2 (square kilometers)	square miles	divide by 2.59
km^2 (square kilometers)	acres	multiply by 247.1
hectares	acres	multiply by 2.471
cm^3 (cubic centimeters)	cubic inches	multiply by 16.387
m^3 (cubic meters)	cubic yards	multiply by 1.308
l (liters)	pints	multiply by 2.113
l (liters)	gallons	divide by 3.785
g (grams)	ounces	divide by 28.329
kg (kilograms)	pounds	multiply by 2.205
metric tonnes	short tons	multiply by 1.1023
metric tonnes	long tons	multiply by 0.9842
BTUs (British thermal units)	kWh (kilowatt-hours)	divide by 3,415.3
watts	horsepower	multiply by 0.001341
kWh (kilowatt-hours)	horsepower-hours	multiply by 1.341
MW (megawatts)	horsepower	multiply by 1,341
gigawatts per hour	horsepower per hour	multiply by 1,341,000
°C (degrees Celsius)	°F (degrees Fahrenheit)	multiply by 1.8 then add 32

Crowds enjoy the sunshine in Cracow's main square, with St Mary's Church in view.

Rolling farmland with stacked
hay drying in the sun.